For Bunu, Dadu, Nani, and Nana

Written and drawn by Aroop Mukharji and Auyon Mukharji

Image and color assistance by Erik Tostevin

Inking assistance by Abe Dieckman

When the President Poops

By Auyon Mukharji & Aroop Mukharji

Everybody has to poop.

Even the President?

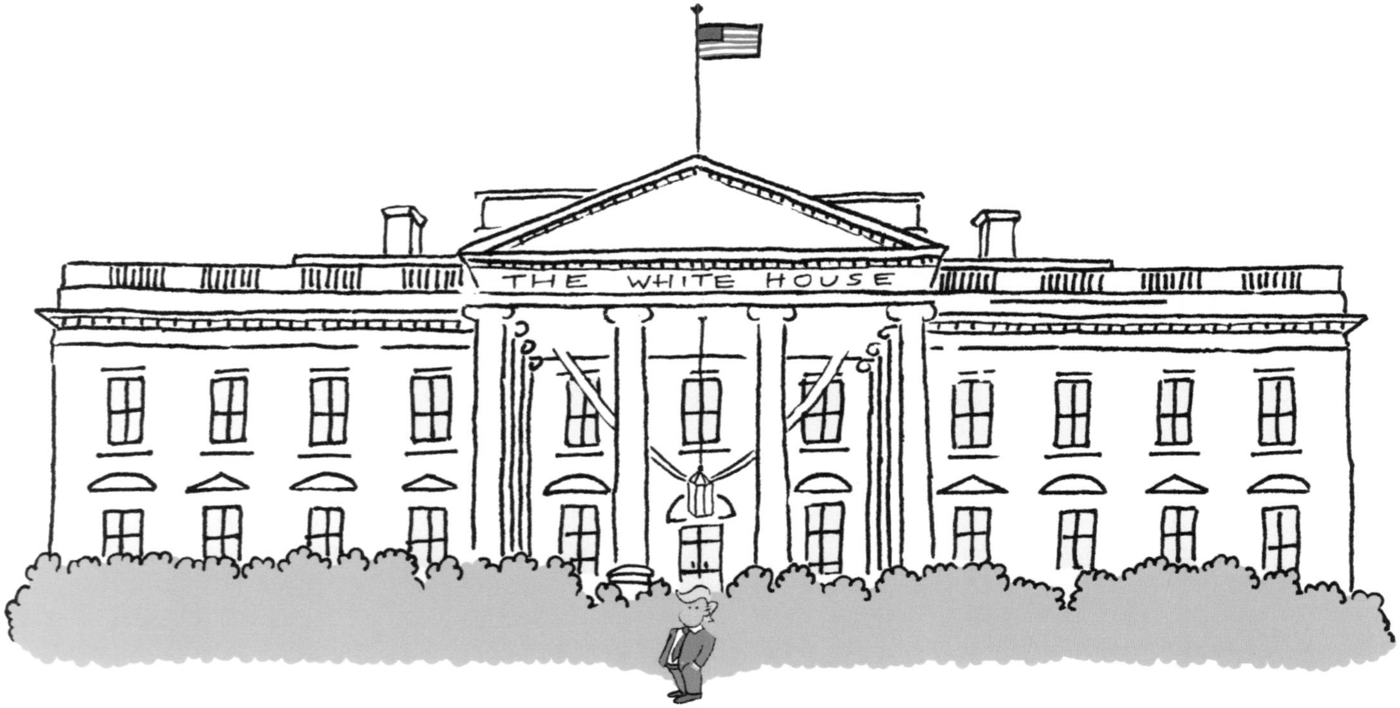
THE WHITE HOUSE

Even the President.

What about during important meetings?

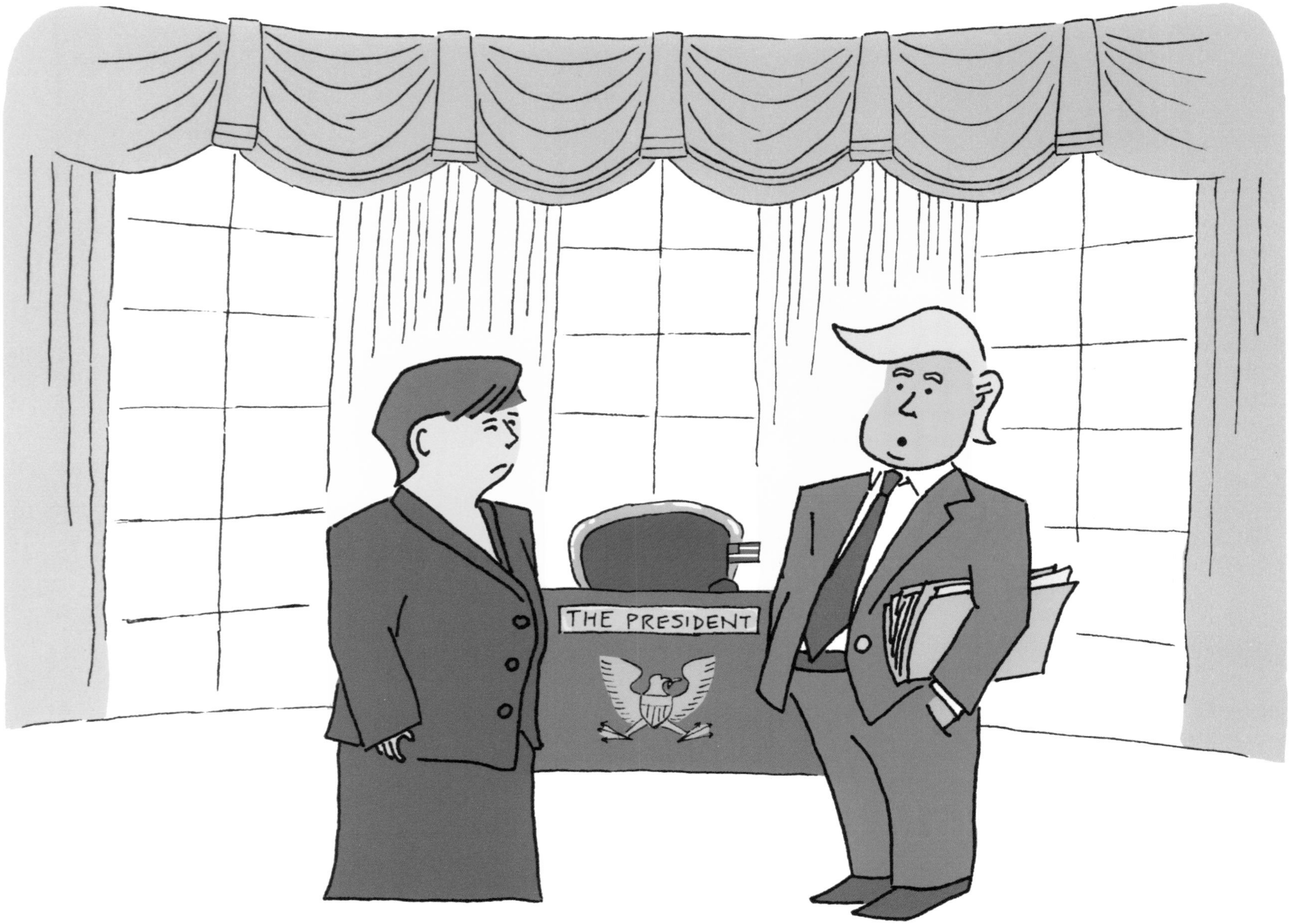
THE PRESIDENT

Sometimes.

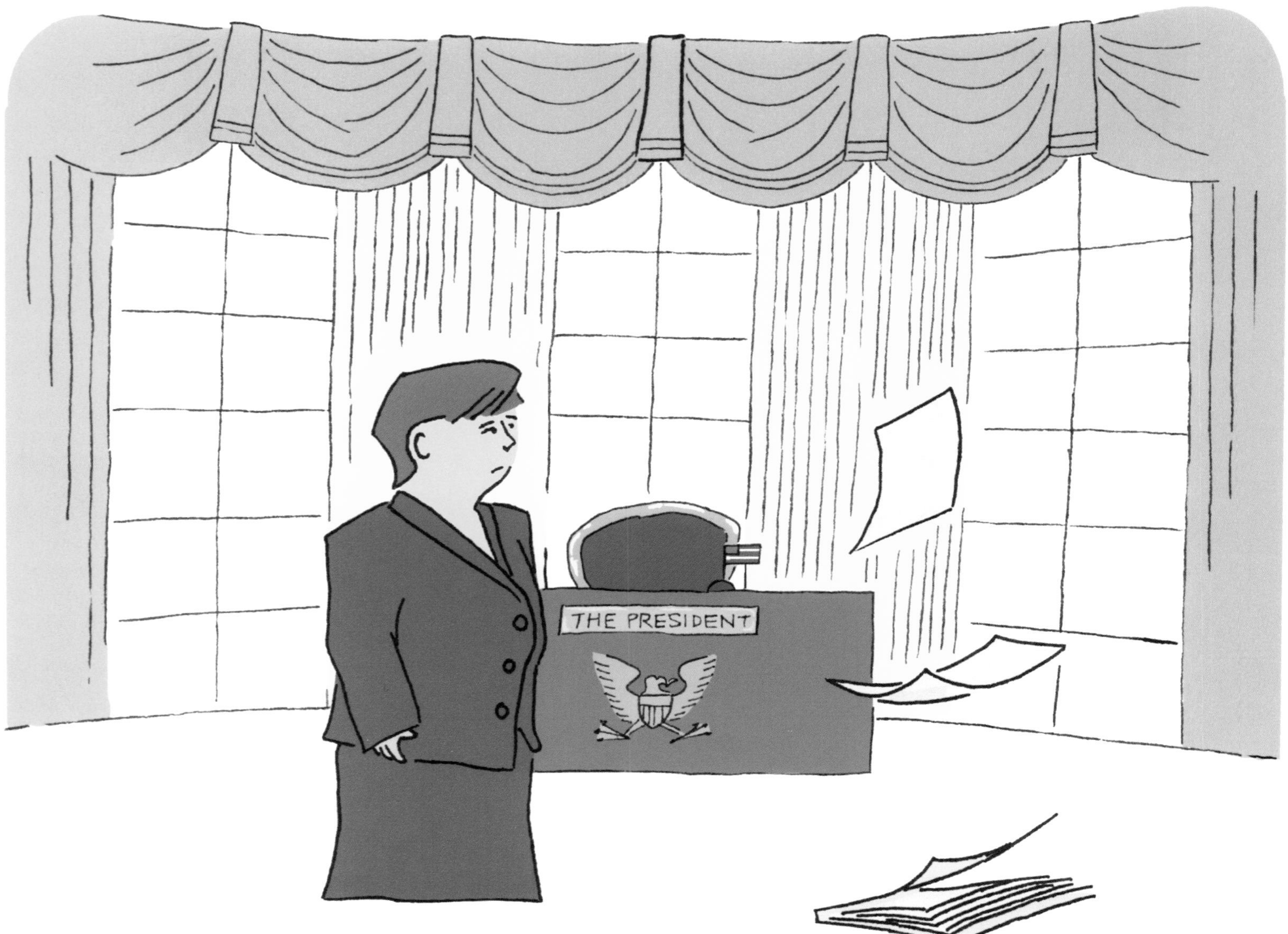
THE PRESIDENT

What about when he is inside his helicopter?

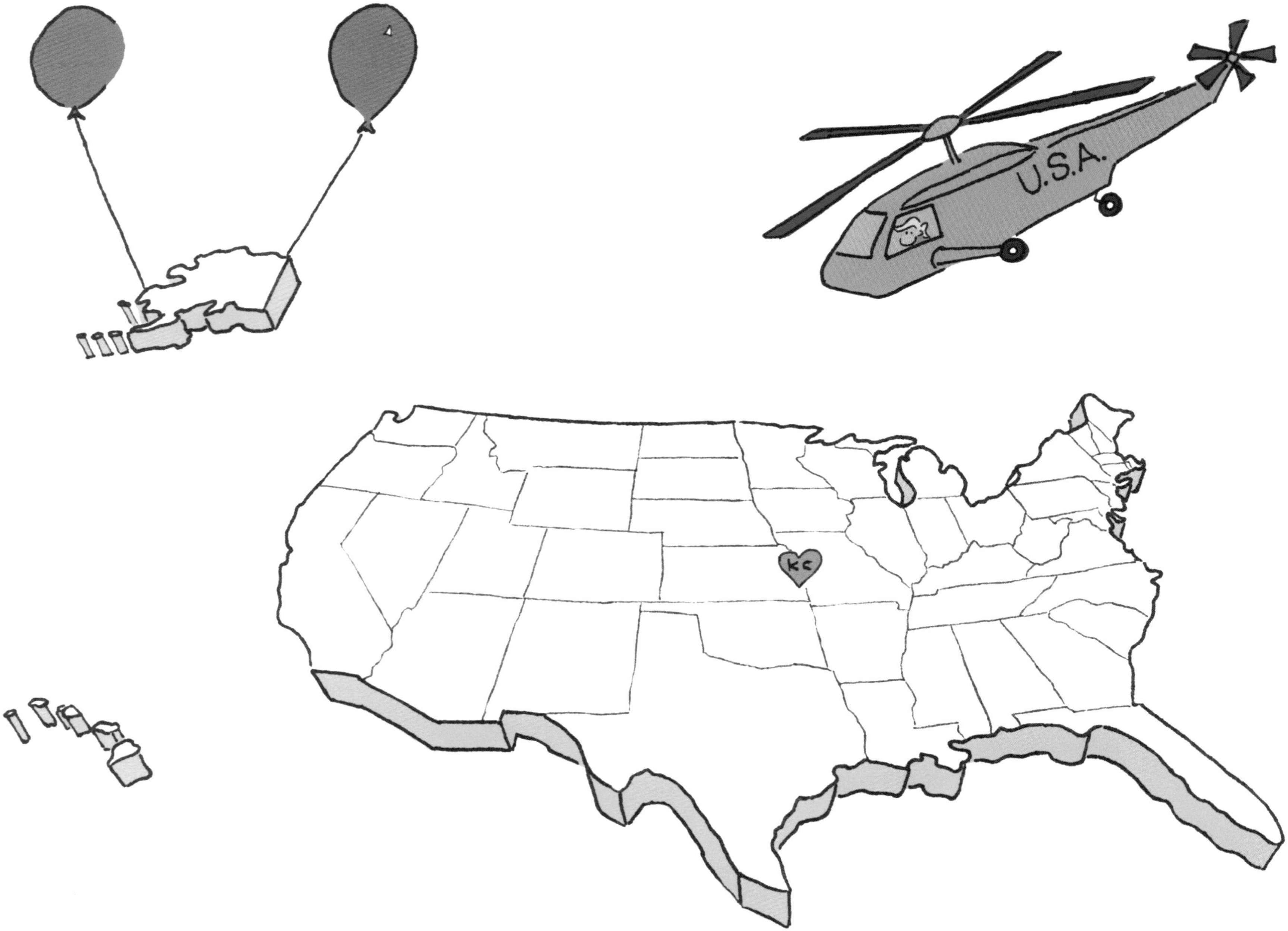
U.S.A.
KC

Sometimes.

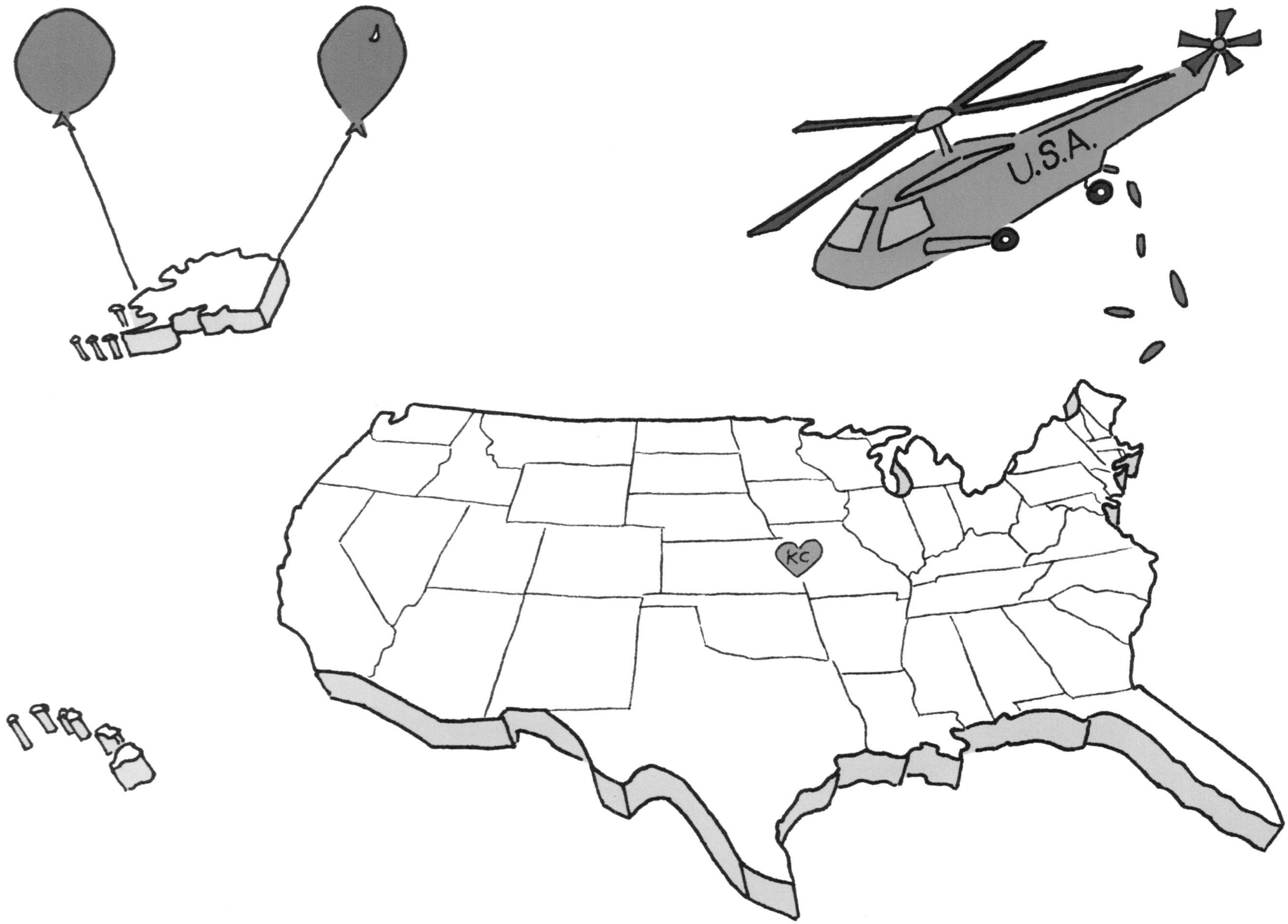
U.S.A.
KC

What about when he is making important rules?

Sometimes.

Sometimes it happens when he is playing golf.

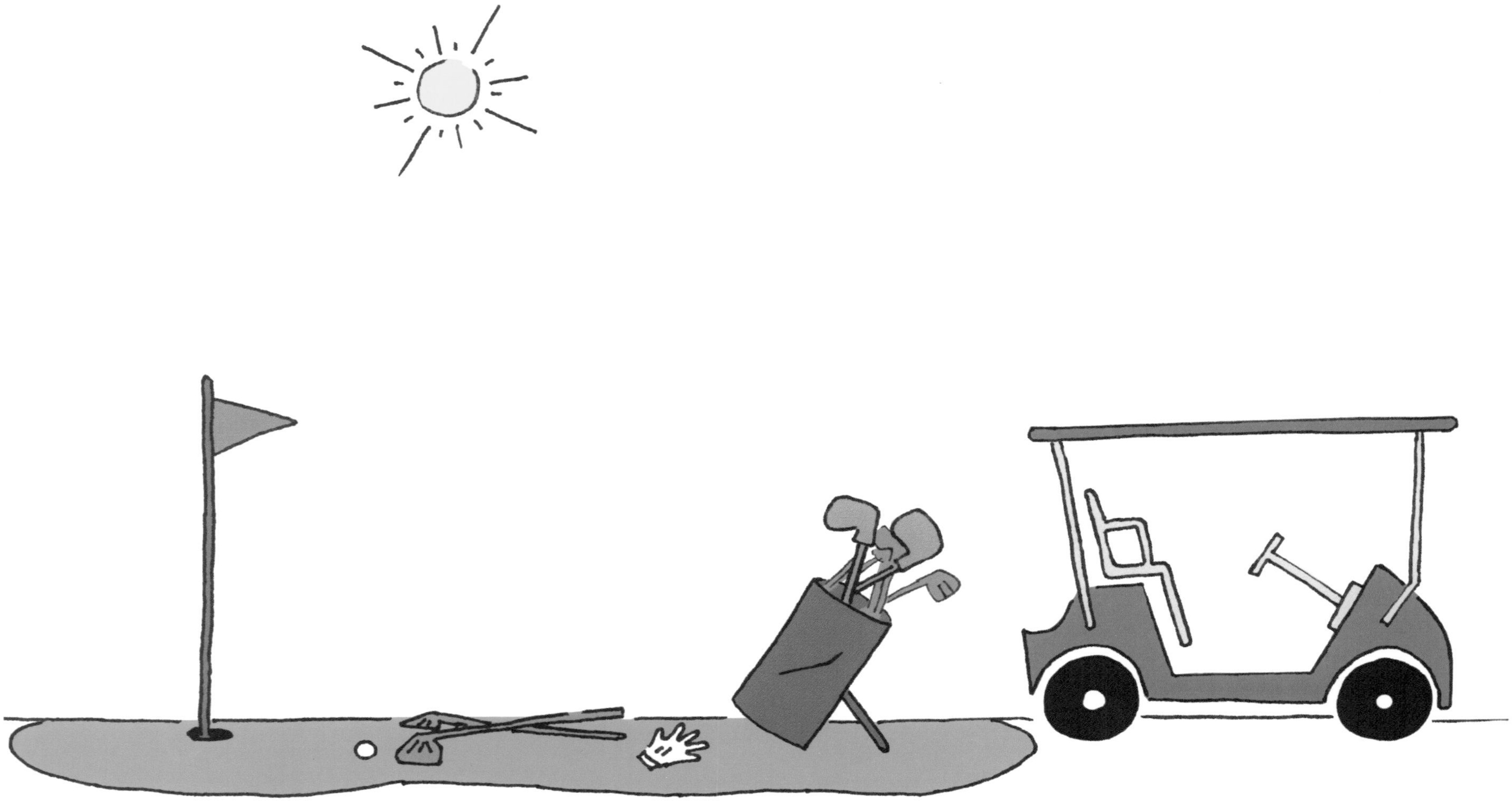

Sometimes it happens when he is practicing a speech.

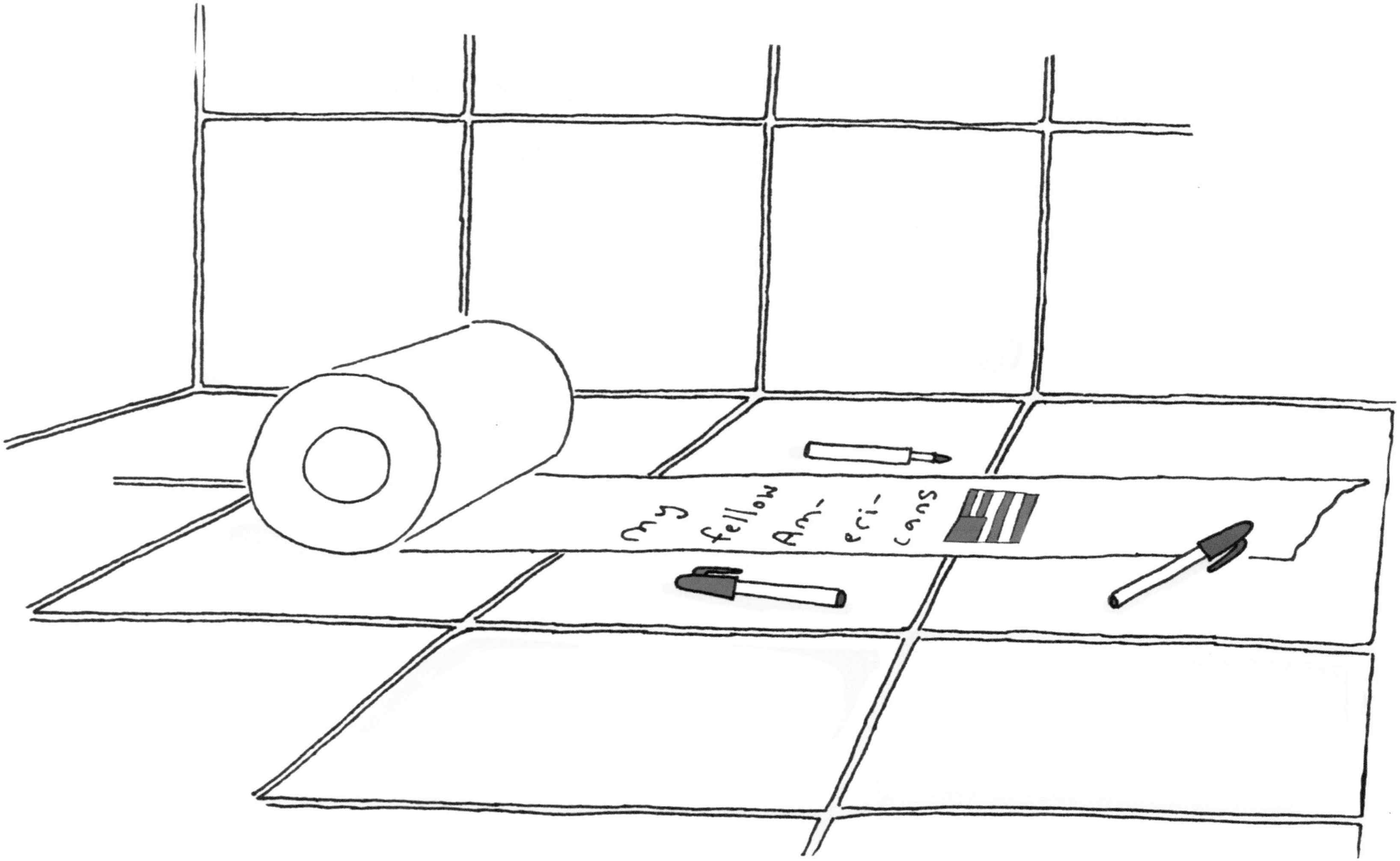
my
fellow
Am-
eri-
cans

Sometimes it happens when he is answering questions.

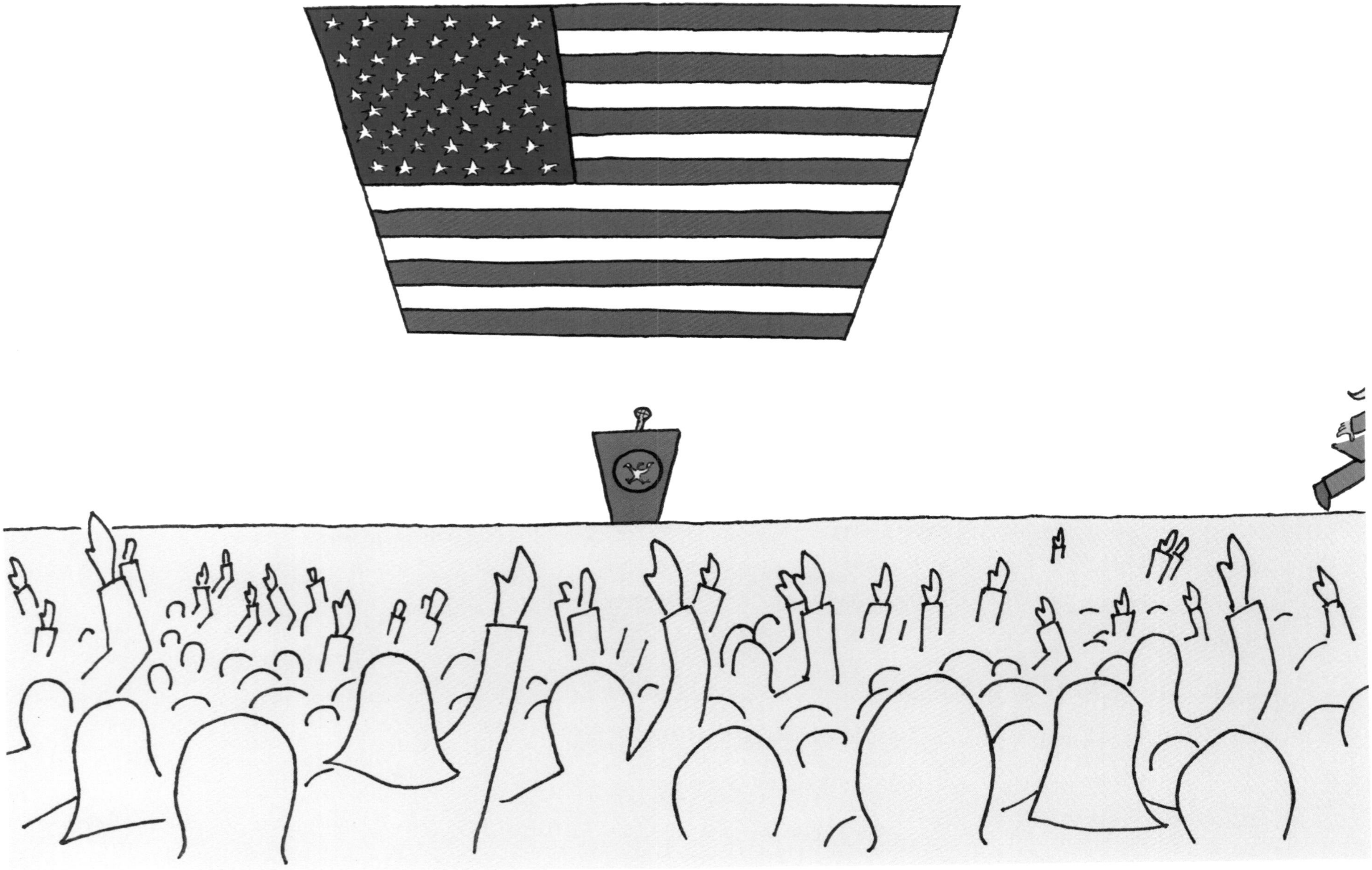

The President is an important person.

But he still poops.

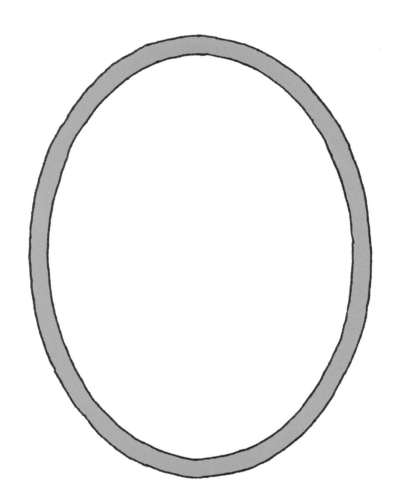

ABOUT THE AUTHORS

Aroop and Auyon Mukharji are brothers from Kansas City. Their older brother's name is Arnob. He also poops.

CPSIA information can be obtained at www.ICGtesting.com
Printed in the USA
LVIW01n2332130218
566525LV00004B/9